Bush Theatre

C000283265

The Bush Theatre and HighTide Festival Theatre
presents the UK premiere of

FORGET ME NOT

by Tom Holloway

08 December – 16 January 2016
Bush Theatre, London

FORGET ME NOT

by Tom Holloway

Cast (in order of appearance)

Gerry	**Russell Floyd**
Mary	**Eleanor Bron**
Sally	**Sarah Ridgeway**
Mark	**Sargon Yelda**

Creative Team

Director	**Steven Atkinson**
Designer	**Lily Arnold**
Lighting Designer	**Elliot Griggs**
Sound Designer	**George Dennis**
Assistant Director	**Andrew Twyman**
Costume Supervisor	**Holly Henshaw**
Casting Director	**Ruth O'Dowd**
Dialect Coach	**Elspeth Morrison**
Company Stage Manager	**Martha Mamo**
Assistant Stage Manager	**Hannah Gore**

The Bush Theatre and HighTide Festival Theatre would like to thank Dearbhla Molloy, Mike Aherne, Timothy Knight, Yvette Robinson, Rob Drummer, Sadler's Wells and Stage Technologies.

Cast and Crew

Russell Floyd (Gerry)

Russell Floyd is best known to television viewers as Michael Rose in *EastEnders* and as D.C. Ken Drummond in *The Bill*.

His theatre credits include *Sir Courtly Nice* (RSC); *Going to a Party* (National Theatre); *The Importance of Being Earnest* (Oxford Playhouse); *Privates on Parade* (Westcliff Palace Theatre); *Dracula* (Hull Truck); *Up and Under* (Swansea Theatre Royal); *Fit and Proper People* (Soho Theatre); *Clockwork* (HighTide Festival); the title role in *Hangman* (Tristan Bates); *Happy Birthday Sunita* (Watford Palace Theatre and UK/ International Tour); *Shylock* and *King Shariyar* (New York and Europe). Most recently he played the Doctor for Russian television, Noddy Boffin in a theatre adaption of Charles Dickens' *Our Mutual Friend* and the role of Bernard in the film *Offensive*, a Jon Ford Production. Russell would like to dedicate his performance to the memory of Martin Pepperell.

Eleanor Bron (Mary)

Eleanor Bron started her career in satire, in the 1960s, alongside Peter Cook, John Bird and John Fortune, and continued in both comedy and drama, in theatre, on screen and on radio.

Her TV work has ranged from *Absolutely Fabulous* to *Play for Today*, including *A Month in the Country* and Jehane Markham's *Nina*. Her many theatre appearances include work at the National Theatre and the Royal Exchange, in Chekhov, Webster, Coward, Shaw, Holman and Sophocles. Her film credits include *Help!*, *Bedazzled*, *Two for the Road*, *Women in Love*, *The House of Mirth*, *The Heart of Me* and *A Little Princess*. She has written two books of memoir, a novel, verses for Saint-Säens' *Carnival of the Animals*, a song-cycle (with John Dankworth) and co-written several comedy series for television. She recently joined *The Archers* and is currently working on a series of short plays in verse.

Sarah Ridgeway (Sally)

Sarah's theatre credits include *The Cherry Orchard* (Young Vic); *Harrogate* (HighTide Festival); *Twelfth Night* (Regent's Park Open Air Theatre); *Sucker Punch* (Royal Court); *You Can't Take it With You* and *The Acrington Pals* (Royal Exchange Theatre, Manchester); *Days of Significance*, *Titus Andronicus*, *Candide* and *A Mad World, My Masters* (RSC); *Comedy of Errors* (Shakespeare's Globe) and *A Taste of Honey* (Salisbury Playhouse). Television credits include *Miss Marple*; *The Crimson Petal and the White*; *The Suspicions of Mister Whicher*; *Satisfaction*; *Call the Midwife*; *Dark Matters*; *The Making of a Lady* and *Holby City*.

Sargon Yelda (Mark)

Sargon's theatre credits include *Light Shining in Buckinghamshire, Dara* (National Theatre); *Teh Internet is Serious Business* (Royal Court); *Incognito* (HighTide Festival Theatre/ Live Theatre/ Bush Theatre); *Moby Dick* and *The Cabinet of Dr. Caligari* (Simple 8/ Arcola Theatre); *The Tempest, Twelfth Night, The Comedy of Errors* (RSC); *Emperor and Galilean, Mother Courage and Her Children* (National Theatre); *When the Rain Stops Falling* (Almeida); *Stovepipe* (National Theatre/ Bush Theatre/ HighTide Festival Theatre) and *Salt Meets Wound* (Theatre 503). Television includes *Zen* (BBC/ PBS); *Compulsion* (Size Nine Films/ ITV); *Midnight Man* (Carnival); *Saddam's Tribe* (Worlds Productions). Film and radio includes *Spectre* (EON Productions); *Dead Cat* (Low Fat Films); *Look Who's Back, The Afghan & the Penguin and The Casper Logue Affair* (BBC Radio 4).

Tom Holloway (Playwright)

Tom is an award-winning Australian playwright. Plays include *Beyond the Neck* (Performing Lines, Tasmania, 2008 – winner of the Australian Writers' Guild Award for Writing for the Stage); *Don't Say the Words* (Griffin Theatre Company and Tasmania Theatre, 2008); *Red Sky Morning* (Red Stitch Actor's Theatre, 2008 – Green Room Award for Best New Australian Play); *And No More Shall We Part* (In Australia, Griffin Theatre Company, 2011 Winner of the Australian Writers' Guild for Writing for the Stage and the Louis Esson Victorian Premier's Award for Literature; in the UK, Hampstead Theatre London and Traverse Theatre Edinburgh, 2012) and *Love Me Tender* (Company B Belvoir St/ Griffin Theatre Company and Thin Ice, 2009 & 2010); *Gambling* (Soho Theatre/ Eleanor Lloyd Productions, London 2010); *Fatherland* (Gate Theatre, London 2011 and Munich Yung Og Radikal Festival); *Forget Me Not* (co-commissioned by Liverpool Everyman and Belvoir Street Theatre and produced by Belvoir, 2013).

Steven Atkinson (Director)

Steven is the co-founder and Artistic Director of HighTide Festival Theatre. His directing for HighTide includes *So Here We Are* (Royal Exchange Theatre/HighTide Festival); *Lampedusa* (Soho Theatre/ HighTide Festival); *peddling* (Arcola Theatre/ off-Broadway/ HighTide Festival); *Pussy Riot: Hunger Strike* (Bush Theatre/ Southbank Centre); *Neighbors* (Nuffield Theatre/ HighTide Festival); *Bottleneck* (Soho Theatre/ UK tour); *Clockwork,* (HighTide Festival); *Bethany* (HighTide Festival/ Public Theater, New York); *Incoming* (Latitude Festival/ HighTide

Festival); *Dusk Rings A Bell* (Watford Palace Theatre/ HighTide Festival); *Lidless* (Trafalgar Studios/ HighTide Festival); *Muhmah* (HighTide Festival) and *The Pitch* (Latitude Festival). Other direction includes *Chicken* (Paines Plough Roundabout); *Three Card Trick* (Liverpool Everyman & Playhouse); *The Afghan and the Penguin* (BBC Radio 4); *Freedom Trilogy* (Hull Truck Theatre) and *Sexual Perversity in Chicago* (Edinburgh Festival).

Lily Arnold (Designer)

Lily Arnold is a Set and Costume Designer who trained at Wimbledon College of Art.

Theatre and opera credits include *The Solid Life of Sugar Water* (Graeae); *So Here We Are* (HighTide/ Royal Exchange); *The Jew of Malta, King Lear, Taming of the Shrew, The Rape of Lucrece* (RSC); *Tomcat* (Southwark Playhouse); *Beached* (Marlowe Theatre/ Soho); *The Edge of our Bodies, Gruesome Playground Injuries* (Gate Theatre); *peddling* (HighTide/ Arcola); *Minotaur* (Polka Theatre); *Yellow Face* (Park Theatre/ Temporary Theatre); *The Boss of it All* (Assembly Roxy/ Soho Theatre); *A Season in the Congo* and *The Scottsboro Boys* (Young Vic, Parallel Production); *Happy New* (Trafalgar Studios); *Ahasverus* (Hampstead Downstairs) and *A Midsummer Night's Dream* (Cambridge Arts Theatre).

Elliot Griggs (Lighting Designer)

Elliot Griggs trained at RADA.

Recent lighting designs include *Pomona* (National Theatre/ Royal Exchange/ Orange Tree Theatre); *Chicken* (Eastern Angles); *Tether* (Edinburgh Festival); *buckets* (Orange Tree Theatre); *Hansel and Gretel* (Belgrade Theatre Coventry); *Deluge* (Hampstead Theatre); *Lampedusa* (Soho Theatre/ HighTide Festival/ Unity Theatre, Liverpool); *Contact* (Bravo 22); *Yen* (Royal Exchange); *Benefit* (Cardboard Citizens); *Fleabag* (Soho Theatre/ UK Tour); *Henry IV* (Associate Lighting Designer, Donmar Warehouse); *CommonWealth* (Almeida Theatre); *Defect* (Perfect Pitch/ Arts Ed); *He Had Hairy Hands, The Boy Who Kicked Pigs* (The Lowry, Manchester/ UK tour); *Marching On Together* (Old Red Lion); *My Eyes Went Dark, Rachel, John Ferguson, Spokesong, The Soft of her Palm, And I and Silence* (Finborough Theatre); *Infanticide* (Camden People's Theatre); *Belleville Rendez-Vous* (Greenwich Theatre); *Meat* (Theatre503); *Lagan* (Oval House Theatre); *Love Re:Imagined* (Only Connect) and *Folk Contraption* (Southbank Centre).

Awards: Best Lighting Designer (Off West End Awards 2014); New Talent in Entertainment Lighting (Association of Lighting Designers 2014); Francis Reid Award (Association of Lighting Designers 2011); Showlight Award (NSDF 2009).

George Dennis (Sound Designer)

George's theatre credits include *The Homecoming* (Trafalgar Studios); *Primetime, Fireworks, Liberian Girl* (Royal Court); *Brave New World, Regeneration* (Royal and Derngate/ Touring Consortium); *Harrogate* (HighTide Festival); *Chicken* (Eastern Angles/ Paines Plough); *Image of an Unknown Young Woman, Eclipsed, The Edge of our Bodies, Dances of Death* (Gate Theatre); *Beautiful Thing* (Arts Theatre/ UK Tour); *A Breakfast of Eels, The Last Yankee* (Print Room); *peddling* (Arcola Theatre/ 59E59, New York/ HighTide Festival); *Visitors* (Bush Theatre); *Mametz* (National Theatre of Wales); *Minotaur* (Polka Theatre/ Clwyd Theatr Cymru); *Spring Awakening* (Headlong); *The Island* (Young Vic); *Love Your Soldiers* (Sheffield Crucible Studio); *Thark* (Park Theatre); *Moth* (Bush Theatre/ HighTide Festival); *Liar Liar* (Unicorn Theatre); *Good Grief* (Theatre Royal Bath/ UK Tour); *The Seven Year Itch* (Salisbury Playhouse); *When Did You Last See My Mother?* (Trafalgar Studios 2); *The Living Room* (Jermyn Street Theatre); *Debris, The Seagull, The Only True History of Lizzie Finn* (Southwark Playhouse); *A Life* and *Foxfinder* (Finborough Theatre).

Andrew Twyman (Assistant Director)

Andrew Twyman is currently the Artistic Director at Plane Paper Theatre Company and works as a reader for the Finborough Literary Department. His credits include *Forget Me Not* (Bush Theatre, Assistant Director); *A Further Education* (Hampstead Theatre, Assistant Director); *Odd Shaped Balls* (Edinburgh Fringe, Space UK); *Reason and Force* (Kings Head Theatre) and *Fair Exchange* (Tabard Theatre). As Associate, *King of the Fuckin' Castle* (VAULT Festival). Andrew was also a member of the Live Theatre's writing programme and has assisted on workshops at the International Acting Academy.

Bush
Theatre
We make theatre for London. Now.

The Bush is a world-famous home for new plays and an internationally renowned champion of playwrights. We discover, nurture and produce the best new writers from the widest range of backgrounds from our home in a distinctive corner of west London.

The Bush has won over 100 awards and developed an enviable reputation for touring its acclaimed productions nationally and internationally.

We are excited by exceptional new voices, stories and perspectives – particularly those with contemporary bite which reflect the vibrancy of British culture now.

Now located in a recently renovated library building on the Uxbridge Road in the heart of Shepherd's Bush, the theatre houses a 144-seat auditorium, rehearsal rooms and a lively café bar.

bushtheatre.co.uk

" **A powerhouse of new writing** "
- Sunday Times Culture

Bush Theatre

THANK YOU
TO OUR SUPPORTERS

The Bush Theatre would like to extend a very special Thank You to the following Star Supporters, Corporate Members and Trusts & Foundations whose valuable contributions help us to nurture, develop and present some of the brightest new literary stars and theatre artists.

LONE STAR

Eric Abraham
Gianni Alen-Buckley
Michael Alen-Buckley
Rafael & Anne-Helene Biosse Duplan
Garvin & Steffanie Brown
Siri & Rob Cope
Alice Findlay
Aditya Mittal
Miles Morland
Lady Susie Sainsbury
James & Virginia Turnbull
Mr & Mrs Anthony Whyatt

HANDFUL OF STARS

Anonymous
Martin Bartle
Clive and Helena Butler
Clare Clark
Clyde Cooper
Zarina Funk
Lesley Hill & Russ Shaw
Simon & Katherine Johnson
Emmie Jones
Paul & Cathy Kafka
V & F Lukey
Vera Monotti Graziadei
Charlie & Polly McAndrew
Paige Nelson
Georgia Oetker
Philip & Biddy Percival
Robert Rooney
Joana & Henrik Schliemann
Philippa Seal & Philip Jones QC
The van Tulleken Family
Charlotte & Simon Warshaw

RISING STARS

ACT IV
Nicholas Alt
Anonymous
Melanie Aram
Tessa Bamford
Christopher Bevan
Charlie Bigham
David Brooks
Maggie Burrows
Simon Burstein
Matthew Byam Shaw
Jennifer Caruso Viall
Benedetta Cassinelli
Tim & Andrea Clark
Sarah Clarke
Claude & Susie Cochin de Billy
Susie Cuff
Matthew Cushen
Liz & Simon Dingemans
Charles Emmerson

RISING STARS CONTINUED

Catherine Faulks
Natalie Fellowes
Lady Antonia Fraser
Global Cause Consultancy
Jack Gordon & Kate Lacy
Richard Gordon
Hugh & Sarah Grootenhuis
Thea Guest
Madeleine Hodgkin
Bea Hollond
Caroline Howlett
Ann & Ravi Joseph
Davina & Malcolm Judelson
Nicola Kerr
Sue Knox
Isabella Macpherson
Penny Marland
Liz & Luke Mayhew
Michael McCoy
Fiona McDougall
Judith Mellor
Caro Millington
Ann Montier
Mark & Anne Paterson
Lauren Prakke
Barbara Prideaux
Emily Reeve
Renske & Marion
Sarah Richards
Susie Saville Sneath
Jon & NoraLee Sedmak
John & Tita Shakeshaft
Diane Sheridan
Saleem & Alexandra Siddiqi
Brian Smith
Nick Starr
Ed Vaizey
Marina Vaizey
Francois & Arrelle von Hurter
Trish Wadley
Amanda Waggott
Sir Robert & Lady Wilson
Peter Wilson-Smith & Kat Callo
Alison Winter

CORPORATE MEMBERS

LEADING LIGHT
Winton Capital Management

LIGHTBULB
The Agency (London) Ltd

SPONSORS & SUPPORTERS

Drama Centre London
Kudos Film & TV
MAC Cosmetics
Markson Pianos
Nick Hern Books
Finlay Brewer
The Groucho Club
The Law Society
Simon Gray Award
Waitrose Community Matters
West 12 Shopping & Leisure Centre

TRUSTS AND FOUNDATIONS

The Andrew Lloyd Webber Foundation
The Austin and Hope Pilkington Trust
BBC Performing Arts Fund
The Bruce Wake Charitable Trust
The City Bridge Trust
The Daisy Trust
The D'Oyly Carte Charitable Trust
EC&O Venues Charitable Trust
The Equity Charitable Trust
Fidelio Charitable Trust
Fidelity UK Foundation
Garfield Weston Foundation
Garrick Charitable Trust
The Gatsby Charitable Foundation
The Goldsmiths' Company
Hammersmith United Charities
The Idlewild Trust
Japan Foundation
John Lyon's Charity
The J Paul Getty Jnr Charitable Trust
The John Thaw Foundation
The Leche Trust
The Leverhulme Trust
The Martin Bowley Charitable Trust
The Monument Trust
Pilgrim Trust
The Portrack Charitable Trust
Royal Victoria Hall Foundation
Sita Trust
The Theatres Trust
The Thistle Trust
The Williams Charitable Trust
Western Riverside Environmental Fund
The Worshipful Company of Grocers

PUBLIC FUNDING

If you are interested in finding out how to be involved, please visit the 'Support Us' section of www.bushtheatre.co.uk, email development@bushtheatre.co.uk or call 020 7743 3584

HighTide Festival Theatre

A major platform for new writing

- The Stage

HighTide Festival Theatre, one of the UK's leading theatre companies, is focussed on the production of new plays and developing emerging playwrights. Our core work is producing an annual Festival in Suffolk of world and UK premiere productions. We have a national and international profile built from touring new productions to some of the world's leading theatres.

Led since 2007 by co-founding Artistic Director Steven Atkinson, we have premiered over fifty major productions by playwrights including Adam Brace, Luke Barnes, Elinor Cook, E V Crowe, Ella Hickson, Sam Holcroft, Joel Horwood, Anders Lustgarten, Vinay Patel, Nick Payne, Jack Thorne, and Frances Ya-Chu Cowhig.

Every script that we receive from around the world is read by our Artistic Director and Associates. The most promising of these playwrights occupy HighTide's year-round artistic development work, from workshops to full productions. Lansons host our administrative offices in-kind within their Clerkenwell offices in a multi-award winning partnership between a private business and an arts charity.

HighTide Festival Theatre is a National Portfolio Organisation of Arts Council England.

For this production, HighTide is supported by

LANSONS
Advice Ideas Results

The Richard Carne Trust

RVH
ROYAL VICTORIA HALL
FOUNDATION

Supported using public funding by
ARTS COUNCIL
ENGLAND

HT
2015

Our ninth season commenced with the transfer of Vinay Patel's *True Brits* to London's VAULT Festival. Harry Melling's debut play *peddling* transferred to the Arcola Theatre following its run off-Broadway and at HighTide Festival 2014.

Anders Lustgarten's *Lampedusa* premiered at Soho Theatre ahead of its transfer to HighTide Festival 2015 and Unity Theatre Liverpool.

HighTide Festival 2015 premiered new productions by E V Crowe, Anders Lustgarten, Luke Norris and Al Smith, and artist talks with Sir Richard Eyre, Meera Syal and Vanessa Redgrave.

Luke Norris' Bruntwood Prize-winning play *So Here We Are* premiered at HighTide Festival 2015 ahead of transferring to the Royal Exchange Theatre, Manchester.

E V Crowe's *BRENDA* premiered at HighTide Festival 2015 before transferring to The Yard Theatre, London.

Tom Holloway's *Forget Me Not* received its European Premiere at the Bush Theatre in December 2015.

For full details, visit hightide.org.uk

Image: Nobby Clark

Support HighTide

HighTide Festival Theatre is a registered charity and every year the generosity of individuals, corporate sponsors, public funders, trusts and foundations enable us to create our award-winning artistic programme and expand our opportunities for young people.

If you enjoy our work or share our values and would like to support us, please do donate. Your support will help us to continue discovering, producing and championing the most promising emerging playwrights. To donate, please visit **hightide.org.uk/donate.**

There are very talented young playwrights in the UK, and if they are lucky they will find their way to the HighTide Festival Theatre season in Suffolk. I hope you will join me in supporting this remarkable and modest organisation. With your help HighTide can play an even more major role in the promoting of new writing in the UK.

- Lady Susie Sainsbury, Backstage Trust

Supporters

We have important relationships with trusts, foundations and public funders who support our ambition and excellence, allowing us to deliver a wealth of opportunities for practitioners and participants alike. Working with our supporters we are commited to developing the next generation of artists and audiences. Our supporters for 2015-16 are listed below.

Trusts and Foundations

Lansons; Backstage Trust; Adnams Charity; Britten-Pears Foundation; Esmée Fairbain Foundation; Fidelio Charitable Trust; Foyle Foundation; Garfield Weston Foundation; Harold Hyam Wingate Foundation; Mackintosh Foundation; Martin Bowley Charitable Trust; The Noël Coward Foundation; The Old Possum's Practical Trust; Parham Trust; Royal Victoria Hall Foundation; The Richard Carne Trust; Ronald Duncan Literary Foundation; Scarfe Charitable Trust.

Business Sponsors

AEM International; Bishops Printers and John Clayton; CMS Cameron McKenna; Lansons

Major Donors

Sam Fogg; Sir David Hare; Diana Hiddleston; Clare Parsons and Tony Langham; Tony Mackintosh and Criona Palmer; Lady Susie Sainsbury; Albert and Marjorie Scardino; Rosemary Squire OBE.

Friends of HighTide

Alan Brodie; Sir David Green KCMG; Leah Schmidt.

To discuss supporting HighTide please contact Freddie Porter: freddie@hightide.org.uk

Britain's Child Migrants: An Unwritten Past

Child migration is a little known part of Britain's imperial past. Few appreciate the deep roots of this policy which lasted for over 350 years, from 1618 to 1970, and whose scars endure even today.

It started with Virginia, Bermuda and South Africa, reaching a peak in Canada where nearly 100,000 boys and girls were sent from 1875 to 1925. After the Second World War, destinations included the former Rhodesia, New Zealand, and Canada. Incredibly, Australia wanted 50, 000 children in the first three years following the war in order to boost its population. Mercifully, less than 5,000 children were available.

In all instances, governments, churches and charities were actively involved.

Yet what is a distant past to many is also a recent, living history, with painful memories, to those former child migrants and their families who were caught up in these schemes. Imagine being five or six years old, too young to cross the road, and being sent on a six week voyage to Australia to live in a large, brutal institution. You're told you're an orphan who has no relatives at all. Punishments are plentiful if you break the rules, education is scarce and a hug is as rare as a Christmas card.

Fortunately, not all the children believed the stories they were told about their families or their identities. As adults, some asked awkward questions about where they came from, who they belonged to and why they were sent away. They wanted their birth certificates, they wondered about their nationality and medical history and how to get a passport. They asked for simple, basic rights – how to spell their names correctly and to discover their date of birth and the names of their parents.

Some painful truths finally emerged. These were not orphans but sons and daughters from families who had also been deceived about their fate.

Gradually, after decades of denial, two of the governments involved, Britain and Australia, tried to make amends for these misguided policies which caused heartache on an industrial scale. Gordon Brown's apology in 2010 was a watershed moment for all Britain's former child migrants. Yet, a full, independent inquiry and government redress remain elusive goals.

Clearly, there is much still to be done but time is not on the side of former child migrants or their families.

Public awareness has grown over the years thanks to tireless campaigning by the Child Migrants Trust which started its vital, humanitarian work in 1987 and has reunited well over a thousand families. Recently, the Trust has worked with museums to curate exhibitions that bring the stories of former child migrants to a new generation.

Now, Britain will see the premiere of a play that probes deep into the emotional heart of a family torn apart by child migration. Shipping children across the oceans meant they disappeared out of sight, out of mind for most of us. But here, we hope, is a drama that endures and recalls thousands whose voices were never heard, families whose histories were never written.

Mervyn Humphreys
Child Migrants Trust

FORGET ME NOT

Tom Holloway

FORGET ME NOT

OBERON BOOKS
LONDON

WWW.OBERONBOOKS.COM

First published in 2013 by Currency Press Pty Ltd
PO Box 2287, Strawberry Hills, NSW 2012 Australia
www.currency.com.au

First produced on 24 April 2013 by Belvoir with the Liverpool
Everyman and Playhouse at Belvoir, Sydney, Australia

Published in 2015 by Oberon Books Ltd
521 Caledonian Road, London N7 9RH
Tel: +44 (0) 20 7607 3637 / Fax: +44 (0) 20 7607 3629
e-mail: info@oberonbooks.com
www.oberonbooks.com

A catalogue record for this book is available from the British
Library.

PB ISBN: 9781783199303

Cover design by Richard Davenport

Printed, bound and converted
by CPI Group (UK) Ltd, Croydon, CR0 4YY.

Visit www.oberonbooks.com to read more about all our books
and to buy them. You will also find features, author interviews and
news of any author events, and you can sign up for e-newsletters
so that you're always first to hear about our new releases.

I would like to dedicate this play to The Child Migrant's Trust. But I'd also like to dedicate it to John Hennessey. In fact I would like to dedicate it to every single one of the 3000+ former child migrants and their families. And perhaps to my family as well. And to anyone that has got to have a family or hasn't got to have a family. Everyone, I guess. I would like to dedicate this play to everyone.

TH

Forget Me Not was co-commissioned by Belvoir with the Liverpool Everyman and Playhouse. It premiered at Belvoir St Theatre, Sydney, on 24 April 2013, with the following cast:

SALLY	Mandy McElhinny
GERRY	Colin Moody
MARY	Eileen O'Brien
MARK	Oscar Redding

Director, Anthea Williams
Set & Costume Designers, Dan Potra
Lighting Designer, Matthew Marshall
Composer & Sound Designer, Stefan Gregory
Stage Managers, Luke McGettigan & Eva Tandy
Assistant Stage Manager, Chantelle Foster

THANKS

The Child Migrant's Trust, Ian Thwaites, Margaret and Mervyn Humphreys, John Hennessey, Suzanne Bell, Lindsay Rodden, The Liverpool Everyman, Anthea Williams, Belvoir, Zilla Turner, HLA Management, Rachel Taylor, Mel Kenyon, Casarotto Ramsay and Associates Ltd, Peter Matheson, Chris Summers, Kate Kuring, and all my family.

Characters

GERRY
A man in his sixties

MARY
A woman in her eighties

SALLY
A woman in her thirties

MARK
A man in his forties

SETTING
Melbourne, Australia and Liverpool, United Kingdom

NOTES ON THE PLAY

A character's name with no words next to it (i.e. GERRY:), denotes that character's choice not to say anything, or inability to say anything.

The word 'silence' denotes a shared silence that doesn't come from one character in particular.

No punctuation at the end of the sentence replaces the traditional 'dash' that means a line is cut off by the next character.

Ellipses mean what they traditionally mean.

ACT ONE

SCENE ONE

We see GERRY and MARY. They're in the middle of a very small flat.

They look at each other for a long time, before…

MARY: So…

GERRY:

MARY: So, you're Gerry?

GERRY:

MARY: Is that right?

GERRY:

MARY: Is it really

GERRY: Yeah.

MARY: It is?

GERRY: Sorry. Yeah, that's right.

MARY:

GERRY: I'm Gerry.

MARY: I can't believe it.

GERRY: Right. Well, it is, you know, so…

MARY:

Silence.

GERRY: And you're Mary?

MARY: Me? Of course I am.

GERRY: Of course?

MARY: Of course I... I mean of course I am!

GERRY: Right. Yeah. Of course.

MARY: Look at you!

GERRY: Huh?

MARY: Look at the size of you! You're as big as a grizzly bear! As big as a great big grizzly bear!

GERRY: Oh.

MARY: And as hairy as one too!

GERRY: Hmm.

MARY: A big... what's it. Big Foot! That's it! You look like Big Foot!

GERRY: Yeah, well... You know. Sure. I suppose.

MARY: I should call up Guinness World Records. I've found Big Foot! I've caught Big Foot!

GERRY: Well, here I am, you know. So...

MARY:

GERRY: Here I am.

Silence.

This is your home then?

MARY: Beg your pardon?

GERRY: This is where you live?

MARY: Oh. Yes. Sorry.

GERRY: Nice.

MARY: My Buckingham Palace.

GERRY looks around the tiny flat. It's not a nice home.

GERRY: Right. Nice. It's real...

MARY: I know. More like the Tower, right? Or a dungeon. Or some kind of...

GERRY looks back at MARY. They look at each other, neither knowing what to say.

Silence.

A cup of tea. What am I doing? I'll put the kettle on, shall I?

GERRY: Oh.

MARY: Please, Gerry. Have a seat and I'll make a pot. If there's one thing better than a cup of tea, surely it's a whole pot, don't you think?

GERRY: Sure.

MARY: And we've... Well, we've got a lot to talk about, don't we?

GERRY: Where should I sit?

MARY: Anywhere's fine. Anywhere you like.

GERRY gestures to the sofa.

GERRY: Here?

MARY: Sure. That's fine. Anywhere you like.

GERRY: Okay.

MARY: You used to hate wearing pants. Do you remember that? Even in public you'd rip your pants off and run around naked from the waist down. The number of times you'd go up to a stranger and start a conversation when you were starkers. I mean willy-to-the-wind, stark naked... It was... Well it was...

GERRY:

MARY: You don't still do that, I suppose?

GERRY: Hardly ever these days.

MARY: Wait. Mary? You're asking me if I'm... You do recognise me, don't you?

GERRY: What?

MARY: Before. When you said... You do recognise me. You do know me from...

GERRY:

MARY: You don't?

GERRY:

MARY: Tea. I'll get some tea.

They stare at each other.

Eventually MARY leaves.

Once alone, GERRY looks at the chair and small couch on offer, but still doesn't sit. He looks around the tiny room instead. He looks huge in the small space. He goes to a wall and looks at some photos in frames. There's only one or two and they're old.

As he looks at the pictures, MARY comes back in. She doesn't say anything. She watches GERRY, without him noticing.

After a moment she leaves again.

GERRY looks to the door MARY has just left from then moves back to the middle of the room. He looks at the chairs again, then at the front door. After a moment he moves towards the front door to leave, but MARY comes back in with a pot of tea on a tray.

Here we are.

GERRY moves back to the middle of the room.

A good, strong pot of tea. Nothing posh. I hope that's…

She looks up at GERRY.

You haven't sat down.

GERRY: No.

MARY: You should.

GERRY: Yeah, but…

MARY: What is it?

13

GERRY: I just wasn't sure where.

MARY gestures to where GERRY was going to sit.

MARY: You were going to sit there, weren't you?

GERRY: Yeah, but I wasn't sure if that was okay.

MARY: I said anywhere.

GERRY: I know, but

MARY: So sit wherever you like.

GERRY: Can you tell me?

MARY: What?

GERRY: Tell me where to sit.

MARY: Look at us!

GERRY: What?

MARY: Nervous little nellies we are! Can't even work out how to sit down!

GERRY: Look, I just

MARY: As nervous as pigs at a butcher's shop, the two of us!

GERRY: Just tell me where you want me to sit. This is your place. I'll sit where you want me to sit, so can't you just tell me where I should bloody…

Silence.

MARY: There's fine. Really.

She puts the tray down on the coffee table and then they both sit, almost in unison. GERRY sits on the small couch.

She pours out two cups of tea, adds milk and then hands one over to GERRY.

She doesn't touch hers.

And, you've, ah... Just got in to Liverpool?

GERRY: This morning.

MARY: And when did you get to England?

GERRY: About a week ago, I think.

MARY: You're not sure?

GERRY: Jetlag, they called it. It's all a bit foggy.

MARY: Of course.

GERRY:

MARY: I'm sorry about that before with the trousers and the bear and... How silly of me.

GERRY:

Silence.

MARY: What's jetlag then?

GERRY:

Silence.

GERRY has barely touched his tea.

GERRY: The tea's very nice. Thank you.

15

MARY: So, Australia…

GERRY: Sorry?

MARY: That's where you

GERRY: Oh.

MARY: Where you've lived?

GERRY: Yeah. Right.

MARY: Wow!

GERRY: That's right.

MARY: All that sun… All those beaches…

GERRY: Hmm.

MARY: I saw this show once. On the tele. It was all about Australia. Big sandy beaches… Blue skies… Palm trees and everything. It all just looked so…

GERRY: Yeah, well… Sure it looks like that on TV, but… Well, I don't know so much about that.

MARY: You don't?

GERRY:

MARY: Oh. Right. Yeah. Silly of me to think…

GERRY:

MARY: I can't believe you've still got those bright eyes, though. I have to tell you that. I mean, look at you!

GERRY: I don't mean to… I just don't know what I'm supposed to… Just stop saying those things for a bit, can you?

MARY:

Silence.

Where are you staying?

GERRY: Around the corner.

MARY: The pub? Can you tell me what it's like?

GERRY: My room has a view of the park.

MARY: Stanley Park. Yeah. I thought you might like that.

GERRY: Did you suggest it to the trust?

MARY: Well they asked, so…

GERRY: It's got the basics, you know? That's all I need. Just the basics.

MARY: That's what I was thinking… That it's better to be close than to be posh, yeah?

GERRY:

MARY: I just meant… They told me a little about you. About what you've been through. I just meant it's amazing you still have those lovely big, bright eyes considering everything that you've been through.

GERRY:

Silence.

GERRY sips at his tea.

MARY doesn't touch hers.

So, you've always lived here? They said… Told me you'd lived here ever since…

MARY: Yeah. That's right. I've always lived here.

GERRY: For sixty years?

MARY: Everything else around here has changed. I bet you didn't recognise a thing. They bulldozed Everton years back. All in the name of making it better, they said. Does it look better to you?

GERRY: To me?

MARY: Thinking back to what was here before. Does it seem like it's got better to you than it was when

GERRY: You're joking, right?

MARY: Huh?

GERRY: You think I remember?

MARY: But you must remember something from

GERRY: You really think I remember any of that?

MARY: You don't?

GERRY: Of course I bloody don't.

MARY: Nothing?

GERRY: Jesus.

MARY: This building was just about the only one that didn't go. They tried to kick me out too, but… Well, you

shouldn't just try to wipe out the past like that, and
this is our home, so

GERRY: That's it.

MARY: Oh no.

GERRY: I've got to get out of here.

MARY: My home. Sorry. I just meant this is my

GERRY: I'm going to go.

MARY: Please…

GERRY: I'm tired.

MARY: No, it's all right. Please, I

GERRY: I don't mean to be rude. I can be some times, but
I don't mean to be. It was nice, joking and stuff. It
was real nice, but I just don't really know how to
talk to people, you know?

MARY: I

GERRY: I'm going to go. I'll come back, but

MARY: Please don't. I'm sorry, really. I didn't mean to

He stands. MARY follows.

GERRY: It's just I don't reckon you should have said that
about my eyes. About running around without
my… I don't reckon you should have said any of
that stuff.

MARY: Oh.

GERRY: Because joking… Making jokes and stuff already…

MARY: It's just that there's so much rushing around in my head, but

GERRY: And my life hasn't exactly been like Home And Away, you know?

MARY: I'm sorry, Gerry. I didn't mean to

GERRY: Fucking Home and Away or

MARY: Please. You're right. Sorry. I won't… But please don't

GERY: I've got to get out of here.

Suddenly we see darkness. END OF SCENE.

SCENE TWO

We see the living room of SALLY's house. GERRY sits on the couch with his head in his hands. SALLY, dressed for work, stands above him with a coffee in her hand.

It's the beginning of a hot day.

SALLY: Dad.

He doesn't move.

Dad.

He doesn't move.

I made you coffee.

He doesn't move.

Dad?

He doesn't move.

Dad, I made you some

GERRY looks up suddenly.

GERRY: What?!

He looks around him.

He sees SALLY.

SALLY: Drink this, yeah? It's fresh.

She puts the cup down in front of him.

GERRY: Oh.

SALLY goes and sits down. She doesn't look at GERRY.

GERRY picks up the coffee. He sees SALLY looking away from him. He puts the coffee back down.

Sal, I

SALLY: I was thinking before, when I was in bed... I was thinking about that time you made the stargazer for me. Remember that?

GERRY:

SALLY: Dad?

GERRY: Of course. I

SALLY: I was six or seven and you had come home to stay for a bit and I got back from school to find you here and you told me I couldn't go to the garden, right?

GERRY: Sal

SALLY: Not till it got dark. That's what you said. Then you took me out blindfolded, lay me on the grass and then took the blindfold off. Remember? In the back garden?

GERRY: Please, I

SALLY: You'd made this thing. Like a tent, I guess. A tent without a roof. You lay down next to me, all cramped up because you'd made the tent the right size for a kid and you're a great big giant. You lay in there and told me about ambient light. The streetlights and things. I've always loved that term. You told me how they get in the way of really seeing the stars, so you'd made me this thing for me to try to block out the ambient light. You must remember this.

GERRY: You were seven. We did it right out there. I remember, Sal.

SALLY: And it worked. Kind of. We lay there looking at the stars. You pointed out constellations. My star-sign. You knew where they all were.

GERRY: Scorpio's tale.

SALLY: Exactly.

GERRY: Can you still find it?

SALLY: Of course I can.

GERRY: And your mum made us cocoa.

SALLY: Exactly.

GERRY: I know what you're saying.

SALLY: But do you really think you should mention her?

GERRY: I'm sorry, Sal. I didn't

SALLY: I'm not so sure you should mention Mum right now.
           If you don't mind?

GERRY:

SALLY: Do you know what time you got home last night?

GERRY: Sal, please.

SALLY: I don't mean to bring it up, it's just

GERRY: I know. You don't have to

SALLY: I asked you, Dad. I asked you to stay here where
           I could look after you and you just had to stop
           drinking and we were going to work all this out.
           Together. You could sleep on the couch, drink tea,
           watch the TV or do whatever you want, as long as
           you didn't…

GERRY: But Sal

SALLY: And you know why, don't you? You know why I'm
           asking you to do it?

GERRY: I didn't meant anything, Sal. I just needed a drink
           and then, I don't know what…

SALLY: Sorry. I didn't mean to… I'm sorry if it sounded like
           I was getting upset.

GERRY: I want to explain. I didn't mean to… I want to
           explain so that…

SALLY:

GERRY: Oh, shit.

SALLY: Stay there a sec, yeah?

SALLY gets up. She leaves the room.

GERRY sits alone on the couch. He looks at the coffee. He can't face it.

SALLY comes in with a pile of broken picture frames. She puts them on the table in front of GERRY.

Do you remember this?

GERRY: Jesus.

SALLY: Do you remember throwing these everywhere? These are my pictures of Mum, Dad. This is my one picture of all of us. I just set them up a few days ago. Do you remember throwing them all off the side table by the front door last night?

GERRY: I'll fix them. I'll go and

SALLY: Fix them?

GERRY: I'll get new frames. I'll

SALLY: How?

GERRY: I'll do it today. I'll

SALLY: You'll buy new frames?

GERRY: Yeah.

SALLY: Do you have any money left from what I gave you?

GERRY: Sal, I

SALLY: Do you?

GERRY:

SALLY: No. Right. Of course not. Silly me.

GERRY: I'm sorry, Sal. Really. I didn't mean to

SALLY: Can you drink the coffee at least? Please? I made it for you, Dad.

          GERRY takes a drink of the coffee.

          SALLY watches him struggle with it.

          You're still going to go today though, right?

GERRY: What?

SALLY: You're still going to the appointment?

GERRY: Oh, Sal. I don't reckon… I don't know if today is…

SALLY:

GERRY: Shit. I'm such an idiot.

SALLY: Where were you all night? Where do you go? What do you do? How do you get like that?

GERRY: Please. I'm sorry. I just

SALLY: The things you said to me, Dad. The things you said were… Do you know how scary you are when you're like that?

GERRY:

SALLY: Sorry, that's cruel to say. I shouldn't… I have to go to work. I'm late. There's a new head nurse and she's really

GERRY: I'll be there. I promise.

SALLY: You will?

GERRY: I know it's what you want.

SALLY: But that's not why…

GERRY:

SALLY: Thank you. That's… Right. Great. I'll come back
           and pick you up then?

GERRY: Last night… I didn't mean… I just

SALLY: There's no alcohol in the house, so please don't try
           to… You should rest. Pull the couch out. Turn the
           air conditioning on if it gets too hot. And there's
           some food in the fridge. I stocked it yesterday for
           you. Just get some sleep and look after yourself and
           try to be ready, all right?

GERRY:

SALLY: Right. I better…

GERRY:

SALLY: Dad, I…

GERRY: I'm sorry, Sal. I didn't mean to

SALLY: I'll see you later then.

           *SALLY leaves. GERRY sits alone. He looks at the broken
           pictures.*

           Suddenly we see darkness.

           END OF SCENE.

SCENE THREE.

We see GERRY and MARK. They're in a room that looks a lot like a homely living room, but with no TV.

GERRY stands next to a small couch.

It is hot. There is a fan slowly rotating in the corner.

There is a long silence, before...

GERRY: Who do you work for then?

MARK: Sorry?

GERRY: The Government? Is that it?

MARK: Oh.

GERRY: The British or the Australian Government? Is that the game?

MARK: Not at all. I don't work for

GERRY: Don't tell me it's a church then? The Catholics, or... I don't care which one it is, but you should probably fess up now if the church is behind this little bloody façade.

MARK: Façade?

GERRY: Because you charities... I know how you charities work. Being a cover for the suits or the cloth. Trying to hide your old sins. All your disgusting, dirty little... If the Government or the church is behind this... Yes... Façade, then I might as well just leave you to

MARK scoffs.

GERRY: Did you just laugh?

MARK: Sorry. No.

GERRY: At me?

MARK: I smiled. It was just… I just smiled.

GERRY: Why?

MARK: You're right. I'm sorry. Let's start again, can we? Let's pretend nothing's happened yet. It was my mistake.

GERRY:

MARK: I promise.

GERRY looks around the room.

GERRY: I get it.

MARK: What's that?

GERRY: I get why you do all this. How you make it look like a home. It's on purpose, right? To make it feel cosy. Comfortable. The paintings… The carpet… The… Yeah, the lighting too. Like a home. It's all very clever of you. You could get some air conditioning though. Don't you think you should get some bloody… or is that on purpose too? To keep us unsettled?

MARK: I can assure you I don't work for a church or for a government and I'm not trying to get you unsettled. All right? It's too hot to keep this up, isn't it?

GERRY: Too hot?

MARK: Especially here in Melbourne. When it gets like this it's like you can't breathe, yeah? When there's no breeze like this, and with all the crappy concrete, it's stifling isn't it?

GERRY: Stifling?

MARK: The air conditioner's just plain broken, sorry. Trust me, I'd give my right nut to have it working. But everything else... Well, you're spot on about that. We set it all up so you can be comfortable. Is there anything wrong with that?

GERRY: I... You'd give your what?

MARK: Sorry. You have to excuse me. I shouldn't have said that.

GERRY:

MARK: Take a seat, yeah?

GERRY: You know I'm just here about the travel money. I'm fine. I don't need any... I just want to get some of that holiday money.

MARK: It's not holiday money.

GERRY: You know what I mean.

MARK: We'll keep this simple, okay? Just a basic chat about the family restoration fund and nothing more. I won't try and waste your time and you won't try to waste mine, does that sound okay?

GERRY: Yeah. Sure. No time wasting. Sure.

MARK: Great. Can I get you a cuppa?

GERRY: Huh?

MARK: Would you like one?

GERRY: What does it mean if I would?

MARK: It means that you'd like a cup of tea.

GERRY: Or that I'm nervous? Scared or something? Is that what it means?

MARK: Sure. That's exactly what it means.

GERRY: Yeah. I would like one. Thank you. A cup of tea. Thank you oh so very much.

MARK: Let's not get off on the wrong foot, right? I'm sorry I've had a few missteps, but let me say from the start... I'm here for you, okay? I know you haven't heard that much, but I mean it. I'm here for you and I don't come from the government or a church or any of those people that have hurt you so much.

GERRY:

MARK: Right. Tea then.

MARK exits. GERRY doesn't sit. He looks around the room. Opens some drawers and things. Looks out the window. Then goes back to the chairs and looks at them.

After a while MARK comes back with a mug of tea.

You haven't sat down.

GERRY: The heat. I'm fine with it these days. It doesn't get to me. I guess that's one benefit of being brought up on the farm school, you know? Working for hours in the sun without even a pair of bloody shoes. I didn't wear any shoes for twelve years. Did you know that? Twelve years. This is nothing to me anymore. But you're sweating like a glass blower's arse. You're in danger of turning in to a bloody puddle, you poor bastard.

MARK:

GERRY: I know you said to sit anywhere but isn't there a seat you'd rather I sat in? Don't you have it set up in some special way with the angles or something? Or the way the chairs are facing?

MARK: You can sit anywhere you like.

GERRY: I'm going to sit there. On the couch. I think that's where you want me to sit, so that's where I'm going to sit, because I'm being a good bloody man and cooperating, aren't I? Please, your honour, I'd like it stated for the record that I'm effing cooperating with the effing façade.

MARK: Here's your tea too.

MARK hands the tea over. GERRY sniffs it.

GERRY: Hmm.

MARK waits for GERRY to sit. GERRY eventually sits on the couch. MARK sits as well.

MARK: So, I guess I should tell you a bit about the travel restoration

GERRY: Why do you do your job? Is it because of your father? Was he a bastard? Is that why you do this work? Help other people with their families because you can't face your own? I bet that's it. And it's always about shitty fathers, isn't it? There's nothing as good to blame as a shithouse father, don't you reckon? You know how I can spot the signs of a bastard father from a mile off?

MARK: Gerry, enough.

GERRY: Do you?

MARK: Because you are one?

GERRY: Yeah. Exactly. Because I am one.

MARK: You've come here with your daughter, Sally?

GERRY: Leave her out of it.

MARK: Pardon?

GERRY: You heard.

MARK: Where is she now?

GERRY:

MARK: Okay. I'll leave her out of it.

GERRY: She reckons I must have an aunty or something over there and that I should go and look them up.

MARK: Yes.

GERRY: You've talked to her?

MARK: She told me that.

GERRY: Did she tell you I need all kinds of mental help, or something?

MARK: Do you think she would have said that?

GERRY: I've got no doubt she would have said that.

MARK: Yeah, well… She did say that actually.

GERRY: I said, leave her out of it, right?

MARK: Sure. Yes. I will. You're right.

GERRY:

MARK: So you think you might have an aunty or
           something?

GERRY: I must do, mustn't I? I mean there must be someone
           over there somewhere.

MARK: But no one you know of?

GERRY: My mother carked it and I was shipped off when
           I was four, so no, there is no one that I know of.
           There is nothing that I remember.

MARK: Your mother died?

GERRY: So?

MARK: It influences the research we do. It means we should
           be looking for a death certificate, that kind of thing.
           It's just to help us know where to look to try to find

GERRY: I was put on a boat. Sent out here. Found myself
           in hell and needing to find some kind of way
           of surviving, yeah? I'm not gonna cry and wail
           about what happened to me. I'm not gonna go
           searching for people to blame or anything like that.
           You develop a thick skin, that's all. You look after
           yourself and get on with things. I'm not interested in
           going over any of that shit from the past, all right?
           I'm just here because my daughter marched me in
           here and seeing what a terrible fucking father I've
           been to her, it's the least I could do. And if I get a
           free trip to England, why the hell not, hey?

MARK: Sally said you're from Liverpool. Is that right?

GERRY stands up.

GERRY: Look, you mention her name again... Even just mention her bloody name again and I will... I will come over there and...

MARK: Gerry, I'm sorry. I'm off my game today. Forgive me. Maybe just sit back down and

GERRY: Just find a fucking aunty, will you? You fucking clown.

GERRY goes to storm out.

Suddenly we see darkness.

END OF SCENE.

SCENE FOUR

We see GERRY and MARY. MARY has plates and things in her arms, ready to put out for a meal. GERRY is standing near the couch, not 'in the room' and not 'out of the room'.

There's a long pause.

GERRY: Dinner?

MARY: Yeah, but

GERRY: You made dinner?

MARY: Some scouse. I made it before you came because I thought we might want to eat together.

GERRY: Scouse?

MARY: It's a kind of stew.

GERRY: You shouldn't have done that.

MARY: It's just a stew. It's a tradition around here. Local…
           what's the word? Cuisine. Yeah. But that makes it
           sound far more posh than it really

GERRY: You shouldn't have gone to the trouble, is what I
           mean.

MARY: I'll just lay these plates out and

GERRY: No. You're not getting me. You're not getting what
           I'm saying to you.

MARY: We don't have to eat if you don't want to. It'll keep.
           Scouse could survive a nuclear war. We don't have
           to

GERRY: No. Stop. I'm trying to say… What I'm trying to say
           is…

MARY:

GERRY: Let me. Please.

           He goes and takes the plates from MARY. He lays them out.

           MARY watches everything he does.

           *When he's finished he looks back to her and they stand in
           silence, staring at each other for a moment, before…*

MARY: Do you want a bevvy or something? I thought wine
           might be good. It's Australian. I thought you might
           like that. Help you feel at home, you know?

GERRY:

MARY: Please, won't you sit down?

GERRY: There? Should I sit back there, or up at the table?

MARY: Oh. There's fine. It's still… The whole thing's still heating up, so there's just fine for now.

GERRY looks back at the couch, then goes over and sits back down. He then looks up at MARY, who doesn't sit. They look at each other for a moment.

Sorry… Wine then.

She goes to the table and pours him a glass of wine. She doesn't pour one for herself. She then moves to take the wine over to GERRY, before deciding to take the whole bottle too.

Just in case.

She passes the glass to GERRY, puts the bottle on the coffee table and then sits down.

Cheers.

GERRY drinks. They look at each other. GERRY looks away. MARY keeps looking at him.

Silence.

Is it all right?

GERRY: Sorry?

MARY: The wine?

GERRY: It's good, thanks.

MARY: Do you know it, from Australia? This brand? Label? Whatever you call it?

GERRY: I'm not sure.

MARY: You don't drink it there?

GERRY: I don't know.

MARY: I hope it's not some really cheap stuff that you
        wouldn't normally touch!

GERRY: To be honest, most of the time when I drink, what's
        on the label isn't that important to me.

MARY: Sorry?

GERRY:

MARY: Oh. Right. I see.

GERRY: I can't believe I just said that.

        Silence.

MARY: Could you tell me… I'd like to know a bit about
        your life, Gerry. Life in Australia. Could you tell me
        something?

GERRY: I don't know. What do you want to know?

MARY: What have you done? For a job? What about that?

GERRY: A job? Not much. Labouring mostly.

MARY: Like what?

GERRY: Farm work. That's what I learnt as a kid, so…

MARY: Oh?

GERRY: But farms in Australia… They're probably a bit
        different to here. I worked on this one for a while.

In South Australia. It took two days solid driving to get from one side of it to the other.

MARY: What?

GERRY: That's how big it was. A cattle farm. It was just about all sand and dust. Dust is what I've known most of in Australia. Dust in my eyes. In my mouth. In the cuts in my hands and face. You can get these sand storms that turn the sky red and then... Well, I don't know.

MARY: And that's what you've done most of your life?

GERRY: That's about it. In and out of the city, too, but...

MARY: That sounds...

GERRY: Shit?

MARY: Well, yes! Yes it does!

GERRY: There's my daughter, though. I could tell you about her.

MARY: Please do.

GERRY: She's... Well she's the best person I know. I don't know how else to put it.

MARY: What does she look like?

GERRY: Pretty as hell. And smart.

MARY: Oh yeah.

GERRY: I don't know what I've done to deserve her, to be honest. I'm just lucky she takes after her mother and not...

Silence.

MARY: Gerry, I just wondered. If it's okay to… I wondered if you remembered anything from… Anything at all. Now you're here again, do you remember anything from before?

GERRY:

MARY: If you can. From when you were

GERRY: I don't know what to say.

MARY: Anything at all. Big or small.

GERRY: I don't know. I'm not… Look, it was a long time ago, so…

MARY:

Silence.

GERRY drinks.

GERRY: Is it always this windy here?

MARY: Always.

Silence.

GERRY: They said… They told me that the… The trauma of… That's the word they used. It's normal for someone to forget everything from the time before a… Umm… Traumatic… So…

MARY: Oh.

GERRY: I mean, I don't bloody know, but

MARY: I can understand that.

GERRY: And I was young as well, you know?

MARY: Yeah.

GERRY: So to remember something… To be able to tell you what I remember is…

MARY: No. Of Course.

GERRY: Sorry. I shouldn't swear. I'm sorry about swearing.

MARY: No. It's fine. I didn't mean

GERRY: It's just a bit bloody….

         Silence.

         The drinking. I'm not proud of it. I don't mean…

MARY:

         Silence.

         GERRY drinks the wine.

         GERRY looks at MARY, who is staring at her hands.

GERRY: There's something…

MARY: What is it?

GERRY: I don't know. It's stupid.

MARY: Tell me.

GERRY: Maybe I remember something.

MARY: Oh, yeah?

GERRY: Please, don't laugh at me.

MARY: Of course not.

GERRY: A blanket maybe?

MARY: A blanket?

GERRY: Please don't

MARY: What colour? Can you remember?

GERRY: Blue, maybe? Was it blue?

MARY: Yes!

GERRY: Maybe there was a blue blanket?

MARY: Yes! There was! There was a blue blanket!

GERRY: Really?

MARY: Yes!

GERRY: No…

MARY: There really was!

GERRY: You remember that too?

MARY: An Everton blanket. I made it for you! How funny
         that you remember that!

GERRY: I'm not sure, but…

MARY: No, you're spot on. It was this Everton FC blanket
         that I made for you! I mean it wasn't the best…
         I wasn't the best knitter. It had holes all over the
         place and the writing was all wonky, but still…
         That's… Fancy you remember that…

         Silence.

GERRY drinks.

A trauma you say? A traumatic...

GERRY:

Silence.

She pours him more wine.

Everton, because...

MARY: It has to be Everton in this street.

GERRY: Right.

MARY: Blue to the bone, this street is.

GERRY: I get it.

MARY: Don't tell anyone... You can't tell anyone this, but I wear the blue on the outside, but my heart is red on the inside.

GERRY: Liverpool and Everton?

MARY: But you mustn't tell that to a soul around here. I'd be run out of the street if anyone found out.

GERRY: I saw the flags and things in the windows of the other... I saw all the flags and stuff.

MARY: Exactly.

GERRY: And these boys. There were these two little boys...

MARY: Three doors up?

GERRY: Something like that.

MARY: Little monkeys they are. Lovely, but cheeky little monkeys, both of them.

GERRY: They looked like it too.

MARY: Yes!

GERRY:

MARY: Yes, well…

GERRY: I won't say a word.

MARY: Thank you.

GERRY: I… What do they say… My lips are sealed. Yeah. My lips are sealed.

MARY: Right. Yeah. Thanks.

Silence.

They smile a bit at each other.

GERRY: And… Well… If we're going to… What about you?

MARY: Pardon?

GERRY: I know you said before… With the willy-in-the-wind and… But what other things do you remember? About… You know. About me?

MARY: Oh. Well…

GERRY: If you… You know. If you can.

MARY: If I can?

GERRY: Yeah.

MARY: If I can!

GERRY: So?

MARY: Gerry, I… I mean of course I can. I remember everything about you. Every single, little

GERRY: What?

MARY: Of course I do!

GERRY: But how can you?

MARY: How can I? How can I not? I mean everything about you is

GERRY: But…

MARY: Gerry, you were my world. You were my absolute

GERRY: Don't say that.

MARY: But it's true.

GERRY: True?

MARY: Of course it's

GERRY: Don't say that.

MARY: What?

GERRY: You can't say that.

MARY: Why?

GERRY: Well, it's not true, is it? It can't be bloody true, can it?

MARY: Gerry, I

GERRY: So you shouldn't go and say things that are not

MARY: Gerry. My… You were my world. My… You were everything. Everything I ever

GERRY: Jesus!

He stands.

MARY: Oh, Gerry.

GERRY: Jesus Christ!

MARY: What did I say?

GERRY: You can't do that. You can't say that to me when I know it's not bloody true! When it's so obvious that it's not bloody

MARY: What's wrong?

GERRY: Like you didn't… Like nothing back then ever really… Like you didn't just fucking well get rid of me!

MARY: Please, Gerry?

GERRY: I'm going to go. I'm going to bloody… I don't know if this is a good idea. This whole… I don't think this is a good bloody idea.

MARY: Please?

GERRY: Now I'm swearing again.

MARY: Gerry, I'm sorry. Let me explain. Really. Just let me

GERRY: I don't reckon I should be here.

MARY: Of course you should.

GERRY: I'm sorry. I'm sorry for barging in like this. I should never have

MARY: This is your home.

GERRY: I'm going to go.

MARY: But this is your home Georgie.

GERRY: What?

MARY: Oh dear.

GERRY: What did you say?

MARY:

GERRY: Bloody hell. I'm sorry. Really, but...

He goes to storm out.

MARY: Gerry!

Suddenly we see darkness.

END OF SCENE.

SCENE FIVE.

We see GERRY and SALLY. They're back in SALLY's living room.

GERRY stands near the couch.

It is very hot.

GERRY: Well.

SALLY: I don't know...

GERRY: It went well.

SALLY: I just don't know if I can do this.

GERRY: Really. It was no problem.

SALLY: I mean…

GERRY: It went fine. Really. He's a good guy.

SALLY: I thought I could. I hoped I could, but maybe I'm not good enough to be able to

GERRY: I told you in the car. He's a nice bloke. He seemed like a… He has issues with his dad. We had a bit of a joke around that. Him with his dad, and me being… We had a great chat, man to man, you know? And he seems like a really decent

SALLY: I don't know if I can face all this at the moment.

GERRY: You don't believe me?

SALLY: I'm just… I just thought… I wanted to…

GERRY: What's wrong?

SALLY: I'm just a bit upset, Dad. Don't worry about it.

GERRY: Upset? Why?

SALLY: Don't ask that, if you don't mind?

GERRY: Did I do something wrong?

SALLY: I'll just get a cup of tea. I think I probably need a

GERRY: What did I do wrong, Sal?

SALLY: Dad…

GERRY: You think I've done something, right?

SALLY: Oh God.

GERRY: Talk to me, yeah? Tell me what it is.

SALLY: What happened?

GERRY: When?

SALLY: At the appointment.

GERRY: Nothing.

SALLY: That's not true.

GERRY: Nothing happened.

SALLY: You were only in there for ten minutes. Maybe fifteen.

GERRY: Was I?

SALLY: Yes, Dad.

GERRY: So?

SALLY: I wanted to… I wanted you to…

GERRY: That's all it took.

SALLY: Something happened, didn't it?

GERRY: Nothing happened.

SALLY: I hoped we could

GERRY: Mark said he was off his game a bit, whatever that means, but I didn't

SALLY: He said what?

GERRY: But I promise I didn't do anything that

SALLY: I want to believe you, Dad. I really do,.

GERRY: I told you, he's a nice

SALLY: You didn't do anything? You didn't maybe do anything wrong?

GERRY:

SALLY: Oh, I hate saying this.

GERRY: Why would I

SALLY: You didn't storm out or anything like that?

GERRY: Why would I storm out? I didn't

SALLY: You weren't... Belligerent... And then stormed out?

GERRY: Belligerent?

SALLY: Well?

GERRY: I don't know what that means.

SALLY: Dad?

GERRY: No. I wasn't... I didn't... I was nice. I was trying to be fucking nice, so

SALLY:

GERRY: Look, sorry. You're right. No swearing. Sorry. But it just took ten or fifteen minutes, that's all.

SALLY: We had an agreement, Dad.

GERRY: And I'm here aren't I?

SALLY: We had an agreement that you promised me you
          would stick to.

GERRY: And I have.

SALLY: It's too hot to deal with this. Look at me. You're
          making me all…

GERRY: Sal, I'm

SALLY: You went in there, acted belligerently with him and
          then stormed out, didn't you?

GERRY: I

SALLY: Is that what you did?

GERRY: No.

SALLY: Is it?

GERRY: No, I… No, you can't… Sally, I… Please?

SALLY: I set it up for you, Dad. I asked him to

GERRY: Look, I'm here, aren't I? Doesn't that count for
          something?

SALLY: And why are you, Dad? If you're going to act like
          this, why did you even agree to come stay with me?

GERRY: Because you…

SALLY: What?

GERRY: Shit.

SALLY: Because I asked you to?

GERRY: No, I didn't mean

SALLY: Is that what you were going to say?

GERRY: No, Sal. I promise. I wasn't... I didn't... I... Oh, Jesus Christ!

SALLY:

GERRY: Look, I'll call him up. I'll talk to him again. I'll apologise. I'll sort it out. It's just that all this is a bit bloody

SALLY: Tough?

GERRY: There's a lot of stuff wrapped up in this Sal. I can't just

SALLY: You promised me. I tracked you down. I found you in that horrible little club or whatever it was. I told you. Mum... She's... I told you straight out. You promised me you'd be there. I waited. It was just me. No one else. Just me with mum in that shitty coffin because it's all I could afford and this was all... What... A week ago? God! It's barely even been a week since I had to

GERRY: I...

SALLY: God!!

         She stops herself.

GERRY: Sal...

SALLY: No.

GERRY: Let me

SALLY: I'm sorry.

GERRY: Please.

SALLY: That was all… I shouldn't have said any of that.

GERRY: Sal, please, I

SALLY: I didn't mean to… I just got a bit upset. I didn't mean to say any of that.

GERRY: No. You should… You

SALLY: Let's just pretend I didn't. Can we do that? You're right. You can call Mark up and we'll make another appointment. It is tough, you're right. I understand that. I didn't mean to… I'm just finding all this a bit…

GERRY: Please, let me

SALLY: You know, I was thinking. I'd quite like to take Mum's room, I think. I just want to be near her for a while. How about you move from the couch to my room, and I'll take hers. It's silly to leave it empty. But also… I just think I would like to spend some time with her, you know?

GERRY: Sal, I'm sorry. I'm really

SALLY: You're all I've got now, Dad. Do you see that? If we can't get through this, then…

GERRY: Oh, Sal…

SALLY:

GERRY: Sal, I don't

SALLY: What?

GERRY: Look at me. What good am I to you?

SALLY:

GERRY: I mean…

SALLY: I'm going to go and have a lie down in Mum's
          room. Maybe move your stuff in to mine while I'm
          having a rest?

          SALLY hurries off to her mother's old room.

          Suddenly we see darkness.

          END OF SCENE.

SCENE SIX.

We see GERRY alone. He has a cheap bottle of wine and a glass in front of him. He looks at the glass and bottle.

He picks the bottle up and opens it.

He puts it back down and looks at it again.

He pours out a glass.

He looks at the glass.

He drinks the glass in one go.

He puts the glass back down and looks at it again.

He puts his head in his hands.

He looks back up and fills the glass again and drinks it all again in one go, very quickly.

He puts the glass back down.

He stares at the bottle and glass.

He pours another glass slowly.

He looks at it.

He picks it up.

He drinks it in one go, but more slowly.

He looks at the glass.

He stands up.

He looks at the bottle.

He picks the bottle up and drinks from it until it is empty.

He drops the bottle on the ground.

He looks at the glass.

He picks up the glass, pushes its rim against his forehead, and grimaces as if he is about to burst.

END OF SCENE.

SCENE SEVEN.

We see GERRY, MARK and SALLY. MARK and SALLY are sitting. GERRY has just stood up from the couch.

It's very hot. There's a fan in the room, but it doesn't help much.

GERRY: What?

MARK:

GERRY: What did you…

MARK:

GERRY: Sorry, but what did you just say?

MARK: This happens a lot.

GERRY: It does?

MARK: Yeah.

GERRY: What does?

MARK: It's okay.

GERRY: But what happens a lot? What is it you're trying to say? I don't get what you're saying to me!

SALLY: Dad...

GERRY: This is me? You're trying to tell me this is me?! Is that what you're saying?!

MARK:

GERRY: But I'm not... I don't get... How can this be me?!

SALLY: Dad, sit down, yeah?

GERRY: But did you get what he just... I mean do you get what he's trying to tell us?

SALLY: Dad, I know, but sit down with me, yeah? Can you do that?

GERRY: Sit down?!

SALLY: Please?

MARK: Gerry, I have to tell you, we've seen this before.

GERRY: Gerry?

MARK: Yes.

GERRY: But I'm not. You're saying I'm not bloody Gerry.

MARK: Of course you're Gerry.

GERRY: But didn't you just tell me I'm not?!

SALLY: Dad…

MARK: Sit down, Gerry. Sit down and I'll explain.

GERRY: Jesus Christ. I mean… I mean you can't just…
Jesus! Jesus fucking…

Silence.

GERRY sits back down.

MARK: We found some documents we think might be
yours. From a home in England where we think you
might have been, before you came out here.

GERRY: Home?

MARK: Orphanage.

GERRY: I wasn't in any

MARK: They're hand written. At the orphanage there was
no record of a Gerry Connor born on the twenty-
first of August, nineteen fifty-seven.

GERRY: That's because I wasn't ever in any

MARK: But there was a record of a George Connor born
on that date in nineteen fifty-six, so we searched for
that birth certificate and we found

GERRY: No!

SALLY: Dad…

MARK: As I said, this happens often. Too often. Someone didn't read a form right and all of a sudden George becomes Gerry and… Well…

GERRY: Stop, please.

MARK: But I'd bet my house this is you.

GERRY: Can you just stop for a second, because you're telling me… What you're telling me here is… I mean what you're saying is…

SALLY reaches out and holds GERRY's hand. He looks at her, then back at MARK.

What you're saying is the only thing I knew about myself… The only thing that told me anything about myself, was a cock-up? Was because someone couldn't read someone else's handwriting?

SALLY: You… Sorry. You're absolutely sure?

MARK: As I said, I've seen this before. A lot. The similar dates of birth, the similarity between the names. This is going to be your father, okay? Gerry, this will be you. I swear on it. This is your birth certificate.

GERRY: But my name… Who I am… But you're saying that…

MARK: Yes. That's what I'm saying.

GERRY:

MARK: Why don't I give you a moment? I'll step out, and give you both a second, because this stuff is… So I'll just step out and you two take your time, okay? Feel comfortable to take as much time in here as you need, okay?

GERRY: An orphanage? I spent time in an orphanage?

MARK stands.

MARK: That doesn't mean anything bad about you, okay? You had no say, remember that. You were a kid. A toddler even. You were just a little…

GERRY:

MARK: Okay.

MARK gives SALLY a look and then leaves.

Silence.

GERRY: You held my hand.

SALLY: Dad…

GERRY: Why did you do that?

SALLY: How are you?

GERRY: You really did it?

SALLY: How are you, Dad?

GERRY: You held my hand, after everything that

SALLY: This news is

GERRY: It felt horrible when you did that.

SALLY: Dad, not now, okay?

GERRY: No, I don't mean

SALLY: I'm trying to be here for you.

GERRY: No, Sally

SALLY: So don't be like this, please? Try not being like this
          for me? Just this one time?

GERRY: Sally, I mean that when you did that, it felt horrible
          because of all the shit I've put you through.

SALLY:

GERRY: Because of what I've done to you. To you and...
          Because of who I am.

SALLY: You've said this before.

GERRY: I know, but this time it's different, I promise. This
          time I really

SALLY: Normally you'd be drunk and asking Mum for
          money.

GERRY: But that's exactly what I'm talking about.

SALLY: So I don't know what you mean, saying it now.

GERRY: I know, but

SALLY: I held your hand because I... Because what Mark
          just told us was... God! I'm trying to be here for
          you, Dad!

GERRY: Shit.

SALLY: I need to find out what happened to you.

GERRY: Sally.

SALLY: I don't know what you've been through, but I need
           to know.

GERRY: Sal.

SALLY: Mum always said something really bad happened to
           you and I need to know what it is, because I don't
           understand why she kept letting you back in the
           house.

GERRY: Sal, listen.

SALLY: You never tell me. You never say anything and she
           never told me anything apart from 'be patient with
           him' or 'look after him' and I tried but you were the
           adult and I was the... I was just the kid!

GERRY: Can you just stop for a

SALLY: That's all Mum would say. 'That's not him. When
           he's like that, it's not really him', but

GERRY: Let me talk, Sal. Let me try and

SALLY: That's all I've ever known and no one's ever told
           me anything and so how am I supposed to

GERRY: I was there, Sal! I was bloody

SALLY: Now Mum's gone what am I supposed to do about
           everything?!

GERRY:

SALLY: What did you say?

GERRY: I was there.

SALLY: Where?

GERRY: At the cemetery. At the…

SALLY:

GERRY: When your mum… When you… Bloody hell.

SALLY:

GERRY: I tried. I borrowed a suit… Got some flowers… I
         got to the gates… I was right there, but then I…
         The flowers were shit… The suit was dirty and
         didn't fit… I was disgusted. How I looked… Who I
         was… How I'd treated her… How I'd treated you.
         I wanted to be sick. Because I am. I am sick. I'm a
         bloody joke. Pathetic. I'm a pathetic fucking

SALLY: You were there?

GERRY: I went across the road to a pub. I sat there in the
         window and got drunk. I watched you leave and got
         more drunk. They kicked me out at closing. I don't
         know where I went from there. I don't remember
         where I slept. I don't bloody remember any…

SALLY: God.

GERRY: That's what I did to say goodbye to your mother.

SALLY: Oh God.

GERRY: That's what I did when you needed

         She gets up.

SALLY: There was this time when I was young. You'd
         turned up at home. Drunk. Angry. I heard Mum
         letting you in. I heard you shouting and screaming.
         The next morning… In that wall in the living
         room… You'd punched it. I'd always thought you'd
         just punched it. I never put the hole in the wall

together with the cuts and bruises on Mum's face, because you wouldn't… I'd always been told the real you would never… I never let myself believe that what you must have done was shove Mum's head in to the wall, but I guess that must have been what you did, wasn't it?

GERRY:

SALLY: Is that what you did?

GERRY:

SALLY: Why would she let you back after doing something like that?

GERRY: I don't

SALLY: Why would she forgive you for doing something like that to her?

GERRY: Please, I

SALLY: I miss her so much! I had to watch her die! Slowly! Not able to help! And now she's gone and I want to miss her like something has been ripped out of me, but I'm too angry with her! I'm so angry with her and I don't know why… I don't know what to… I don't want to feel like… I don't know how to… OH GOD!

GERRY:

SALLY: You're not the only one in this. You're not the only one trying to deal with all this. You know that don't you?

GERRY: Sal, please. I'm trying. What I'm trying to say is… What I mean is

SALLY: Jesus, it's so hot! I can't breathe! This city! Like it's
           ending. Like you can feel the whole place... I hate
           it! I hate everything! Look at me. Look at what I'm
           doing! Why am I here?! Why am I doing all this?!

GERRY: Please. Please, I

SALLY: You were there? I... I can't believe that you were...

GERRY: Sally

SALLY: I have nothing without Mum, Dad. She was the
           only one there for me. She looked after me when
           I was sick. She came to my concerts or took me to
           hockey. She did my homework with me. She took
           on another job so I could train to be a nurse. She
           did all this. Alone. And then she got sick and what
           could I do for her? Nothing. What could I do to
           make things better for her? Nothing. And now she's
           gone and she did all that for me and all I have for
           her is anger. And Dad... That's you're fault. That's
           what you've left me with.

GERRY:

SALLY: This, Dad. Doing this with Mark. This is how we...
           This is how I say goodbye to her, okay?

GERRY:

SALLY: I've got to go. I'll talk to you later. Later tonight,
           or... Make sure you're at the house by six, yeah?
           That's the new rule. In the house by six, or out.
           Gone. Over. For ever. I'm not putting up with all of
           it anymore.

GERRY:

SALLY: Well?

GERRY: Sal, please. I

SALLY: You make me feel stupid. Do you know that? My whole life you've made me feel horrible and stupid.

SALLY goes.

GERRY sits alone. He looks over the photocopies of the documents.

He looks around the room.

The fan slowly rotates.

He rips things apart, making the room dirty and scattered.

The fan slowly rotates.

Suddenly we see darkness.

END OF SCENE.

SCENE EIGHT

We see GERRY and MARY.

It is late.

MARY: You were gone.

GERRY: What?

MARY: Just like that.

GERRY: How?

MARY: I came home from work and you were just gone.

GERRY: What do you mean?

MARY: I don't know.

GERRY: How was I just gone?

MARY: I didn't know what they were saying.

GERRY: They?

MARY: You'd stay with neighbours while I worked. I came
         back to pick you up but you weren't there.

GERRY: I don't get what you

MARY: All they would say was… I didn't… Gone? Gone
         where? What do you mean he's just gone? They
         wouldn't tell me anything. They wouldn't say
         anything.

GERRY: Neighbours? You gave me to neighbours and then I
         was just gone? Just bloody… That's all you're giving
         me?

MARY: Please?

GERRY: This is just lies because you won't admit that… That
         you… You just gave me away, didn't you?! This
         is all just bullshit because you can't admit you just
         threw me away!

MARY: Threw you away?!

GERRY: Isn't it?!!

MARY: God, no! Don't say

GERRY: Didn't you?!

MARY: Please?!

GERRY: Well?

MARY: I was coming back from work. Every day I looked forward to coming back and picking you up and taking you home and holding you here in my arms, like you were… I mean it wasn't much, our home. Look at it. It's nothing. Tiny. Small and cold and… Well, horrible really. It's horrible. But it was our home. Our…. And then, to turn up and suddenly be told… For these people that I knew were good people… I have always known they were good, loving people… To suddenly be telling me… To be saying… I was scared. I was scared for you. Where were you? What was happening to you? I mean what on earth was happening to you?!

GERRY: And?

MARY: I asked where you were. Pleaded. I needed to get some… I pleaded with them to tell me anything.

GERRY: This is bullshit!

MARY: No!

GERRY: None of this is fucking

MARY: They told me I should speak to the priest.

GERRY:

MARY: That's all they would say.

GERRY:

MARY: That's all they…

GERRY:

MARY: I went to the church. Out of their house and… And I ran. Ran as hard as I… I beat on the doors. Forced my way in. They didn't want me to go in but I forced my way. I found him. He was with someone. In some kind of meeting. I burst in. Where's my son? Where's my... He looked... He excused himself. Embarrassed. Like he was embarrassed. Excused himself from the other person like this was some horrible, embarrassing inconvenience and then grabbed my arm and walked me out of the room. Turned me round and walked me out, like I was... Like it was me that had... Then... There in the hall, he said it. Flat. Like nothing.

GERRY:

MARY: Your son's gone.

GERRY:

MARY: He's gone somewhere... Better.

GERRY:

MARY: That's what he said. Somewhere 'better'.

GERRY:

MARY: Gerry, please. Please, listen. I...

GERRY:

MARY: I was a single mother with no family. I was young. I

GERRY: What did you do?

MARY: Please don't ask that.

GERRY: Why?

MARY: Don't make me say it.

GERRY: I need to hear everything.

MARY: But it hurts.

GERRY: What did you do?

MARY: God, don't make me say these things! Don't make me say this!

GERRY:

MARY: I believed him.

GERRY:

MARY: I believed what he…

GERRY:

MARY: I thought you'd go to a good family. Some loving family. I thought

GERRY: Family?

MARY: I loved you so much. I just wanted what was best for you. I thought a proper family would be

GERRY: A proper family?!

MARY: I went home. Came back here. Sat there. Sat down on that sofa. Just… I don't know how long for. I couldn't move. I couldn't believe what had just happened. I didn't know what I was supposed to… So I just sat there.

GERRY:

MARY: Your eyes. Your smell. Your smile. Seeing you eat. Holding you when you cried. Keeping you safe. Warm. Healthy. Happy. These were the only things in the world that meant anything to me. And then…

GERRY:

MARY: And then you were gone.

GERRY:

MARY: Then you were…

GERRY:

MARY: Please don't run out again?

          They share a very long silence.

          END OF SCENE.

ACT TWO

SCENE ONE.

We see MARK and MARY at the door to MARY's flat. She is very weak. Tubes run from her nose to an oxygen tank that she has to wheel around with her.

MARY: Oh.

MARK: Hello.

MARY: Who are you?

MARK: I'm sorry. Sorry to disturb you.

MARY: What do you want?

MARK: I'm looking for... I'm hoping you're Mary Connor.

MARY: Are you now.

MARK: I'm looking for Mary Connor.

MARY: Are you from the hospital?

MARK: Can I come in?

MARY: You better not be. I told you to leave me alone. I told you to stop coming around here because I'm never going to go in to that filthy place.

MARK: Are you Mary Connor?

MARY: You'll have to drag me out of here by my hair, do you hear me?

MARK: I'm not from the hospital, Mrs

MARY: You'll have to drag me out of hear by the hair on my fucking head, got it?

MARK: Please, Mrs Connor. I'm not from the

MARY: Housing, then? Is that it? Come to tell me I can't live here any more and kick me out on to the fucking street or something?

MARK: No, Mrs… I'm not from the department or the

MARY: I bet your not.

MARK: Please, I just need to

MARY: I'm not Mary Connor. You've got the wrong place. I don't know who you're talking about, so clear off. Just fuck off out of it.

MARK: It's about your son.

         Silence.

MARY: What?

MARK:

MARY: About my…

MARK:

         MARY stumbles. MARK goes to help her, but she stops him.

MARY: Don't touch me.

MARK: I recognise you, Mrs Connor.

MARY:

MARK: I know your son.

MARY:

MARK: George. I know

MARY: George?

MARK: It is you, isn't it?

MARY: Who are you? Who's put you up to this? A joke? Is
         this a joke? I'm an old woman. And sick. I'm not
         interested in your mean, fucking jokes, you cruel
         little

MARK: My name's Mark, Mrs Connor. I know George,
         your son. I'm here for him. On his behalf.

MARY: What do you mean, you know my son? What are
         you talking about? How did you know I had a son?
         Tell me how the hell you know I had a son?!

MARK:

MARY: Well?

MARK: Can I come in?

MARY: How did you know?! How did you...

MARK:

MARY: Come in then. You better come in. But if this is a
         trick... If you're just here to scam an old lady, then
         you won't get out of here without your eyes balls
         and your testicles swapping places, got it?

MARK: Understood.

         MARY lets MARK come in.

MARY: Go on. Have a seat.

MARK goes to a chair and waits for MARY to struggle over with her canister. Once she is there, he sits, and she starts to sit too, but stops, mid-thought.

MARY: Look at me.

He does.

MARY: Say something.

MARK: Sorry?

MARY: Say something to me.

MARK: My name is Mark. I'm from the Child Migrant's Trust. Do you know what that

MARY: You're not from around here, are you?

MARK: No.

MARY: Where are you from?

MARK: Sorry?

MARY: The way you talk. Tell me where you're from.

MARK: Australia. Well, for most of my

MARY: Australia?

MARK: Yes.

MARY: Why would someone come all the way from Australia to look for me?

MARK: That's where George lives. In Australia.

MARY:

MARK: I hope I'm right in this, Mrs Connor. You do have a son called George?

MARY: Australia?

MARK: Yes.

MARY: Is he all right? Please tell me he's all right?

MARK: He wants to find you.

MARY: Find me?

MARK: I can tell you that.

MARY: Swear to me.

MARK: What?

MARY: Swear to me this is real. On your life. Swear on your life this is all real.

MARK: I swear. On my life. Absolutely.

MARY: Come here.

MARK: Sorry?

MARY: Come close to me. Now. Come over here. Now.

MARK does. MARY feels his face. Feels a lot of him. She isn't gentle.

She grabs his jaw in her hand.

If this is a joke I will break your legs, fuck it. Do you hear me?

MARK: Loud and clear, Mrs Connor.

She lets go.

MARY: Go and sit down.

He goes over to the sofa, but doesn't yet sit.

MARY: Why are you here?

MARK: George. He wants to find you. That's what I've been
         doing. Looking for you. For him.

MARY:

MARK: He needs to find you.

MARY:

MARK: I had to make sure you were the right woman first,
         but

MARY: He wants to find me?

MARK:

MARY: Did you say that

MARK: He needs to.

MARY sits. MARK follows.

MARY: I'm not 'Mrs'. I've never been 'Mrs'. Call me Mary.

MARK: There was a scheme, Mary. Thank you. Children
         were sent to Australia. Orphans and

MARY: What?

MARK: And George was one of them.

MARY: Orphans?

MARK: Yes.

MARY: In Australia?

MARK: Yes. That's right.

MARY: What did you say?

MARK: In Australia. And he's been there ever since.

MARY: No.

MARK: Mrs… I mean

MARY: No, you're wrong. Australia?

MARK: Yes.

MARY: No. George went to a family. A good Catholic family.

MARK: I'm sorry to be the one to tell you about this, Mary. But he's alive and safe and really wants to find you.

MARY: My boy went to a good family! A loving family!

MARK: Lots of mothers were told that.

MARY: Told that?!

MARK:

MARY: I don't like this. What is this? Why are you saying all this?! Look at me. I'm old and dying. Why would you come here and do this to me?!

MARK:

MARY: Australia?

MARK:

MARY: All right. Talk to me. Quickly. Tell me about him. Is
          he okay?

MARK: He has a daughter. Sally.

MARY: A daughter?

MARK: Your granddaughter.

MARY: I have a granddaughter?

MARK: Yes. You do.

MARY: No. Stop it. Don't say that. I might be weak, Mr
          whateveryournameis. I might be old and weak but I
          will beat you… I will come over there and… And I
          will rip your… I will… I…

MARK:

MARY: I've got a family?

MARK:

MARY: This flat. This is where we lived together, George
          and me. This is where I've always lived.

MARK:

MARY: Is he here, George? Has he come with you?

MARK: Not this time. And his name's Gerry now.

MARY: I don't give a shit about his name. Are you… I don't
          have a lot of money. I don't know if my son does,
          but can he come? Can you bring him to me?

MARK: Yes, we can. We can certainly do that.

MARY: You can?

MARK: Of course.

MARY: You'll bring him here?

MARK: Of course, Mary. We'll just need to

MARY: George was… Is all I have. Do you hear me?

MARK: I think so.

MARY: I said do you hear me?

MARK: Yes. I understand.

MARY: I don't care what it takes. Bring me my son, mister. My son and granddaughter. Can you do that?

MARK: We can, yes.

MARY: And will you? Will you do that?

MARK: We would love to. Yes.

MARY: You would?

MARK:

MARY: Right. Well. Do it then. And Mark…

MARK: Yes?

MARY: Hurry up.

END OF SCENE.

SCENE TWO

We see SALLY and GERRY. They are at SALLY's home in Melbourne.

SALLY is sitting on the couch. GERRY is standing near it.

It's hot.

SALLY: Dad…

GERRY: What is it?

SALLY: Come here.

GERRY: Sorry?

SALLY: Can you come and sit with me?

GERRY:

SALLY: I need to talk to you.

GERRY: That doesn't sound good.

SALLY: Please?

GERRY: I haven't done anything, have I? I mean recently.

SALLY: Please, Dad.

GERRY: Shit, I have, haven't I?

SALLY: No.

GERRY: What is it? What have I gone and done now, then? I
         thought I was

SALLY: I got a call from Mark. He's in England.

GERRY: You did?

SALLY: That's what I need to talk to you about.

GERRY: You…

SALLY: Can you come and sit with me?

GERRY: Mark?

SALLY: Yes.

GERRY: What about?

SALLY: He flew over last week.

GERRY: But

SALLY: Jesus Dad, come and sit with me.

GERRY: But what does he

SALLY: Dad, sit down with me before I get upset with you!

GERRY goes and sits with SALLY. He waits for SALLY to speak, but she hesitates.

Maybe I should get us some tea.

She stands.

GERRY: Sally…

SALLY: I'm just going to get us some tea. It'll help.

GERRY: What is this?

SALLY: I won't be a second.

GERRY: Has he found someone?

SALLY: What?

GERRY: Did he call because

SALLY: I won't be a second.

She goes to leave.

She stops herself at the door.

Yes.

GERRY: What?

SALLY: God.

GERRY: What is it?

SALLY: He's found someone.

GERRY: He's...

SALLY:

GERRY: Who?

SALLY: He wants us to fly over.

GERRY: Who is it?

SALLY: He's organising the tickets. Probably for the next few days. A week at the most.

GERRY: What?

SALLY: He says time is short. We need to get you a passport, but they can rush them, he said.

GERRY: Who has he found?

SALLY: Jesus.

GERRY: Sal? Who has he

SALLY: Dad…

GERRY: An aunty or

SALLY: No.

GERRY: Then who?

SALLY: Not an aunty.

GERRY: Sally, I

SALLY: I first met Mark when I'd take Mum in for treatment. There was this other guy on the ward. Older. Mark would visit him because he was… This guy was a child migrant too. He didn't have anyone, so Mark would take him in and stay with him. Keep him company. We talked once while making cups of tea. He made a joke and… Well, that's how it started. Maybe six months ago. I've wanted to tell you. This whole time I've wanted to, but…

GERRY:

SALLY: Mum would tease me about it. Asked me who he was. I told her what he'd told me. That's when she said that you… That you were…

GERRY: What's all this about, Sal?

SALLY: Dad, there's something he said to me when I finally told him about you. I should have told him straight away, but I didn't. I couldn't, or… I don't know. Something.

GERRY:

SALLY: He said that in his job… He told me that they've
         found out that lots of people like you, were… Jesus.

GERRY: Sal?

SALLY: That lots of people like you were told their parents
         were dead.

GERRY:

SALLY: Mothers. Especially mothers.

GERRY:

SALLY: They did this to make the children cut the ties to
         home. That's what he said. That's what Mark…

GERRY: But I don't

SALLY: Dad…

GERRY:

SALLY: Dad, are you listening?

GERRY:

SALLY: Can you look at me?

         He looks at her.

         He's found your mother, Dad.

GERRY:

SALLY: He's met your mother.

GERRY:

SALLY: He's booking us tickets to fly over.

GERRY: Met?

SALLY: Yeah.

GERRY: But…

SALLY: I know.

GERRY:

SALLY: She's sick. Very. That's why we need to get there as soon as we can.

GERRY:

SALLY: Oh, Dad…

He sits, frozen.

Almost despite herself, SALLY goes to him and holds his hand again.

He looks at her.

GERRY: Sal… What do we do?

SALLY:

END OF SCENE.

SCENE THREE

We see GERRY and MARY in her flat. They are at the table, standing.

GERRY: Are you going to sit with me?

MARY: Yes. Of course. Of course I am.

GERRY sits. She doesn't. She just looks at him.

GERRY: What is it?

MARY: I have something for you. I won't be a moment.

She stands and heads back to the kitchen.

GERRY sits silently.

MARY comes back in with a birthday cake.

GERRY: What's this?

MARY: A birthday cake.

GERRY:

MARY: I wasn't sure what you liked. Flavours and things.
           So I went for chocolate.

GERRY: You made this?

MARY: Yeah.

GERRY: But it's not my birthday.

MARY: Does that matter?

GERRY:

MARY: That doesn't matter.

GERRY: Why did you do this?

MARY: I've done it. Did it every year.

GERRY: I've never had one.

MARY: Never?

GERRY: I didn't... I was about twenty and in Sydney for
         the first time and I walked past this shop. This
         cake shop. In the window was a cake with Happy
         Birthday written on it. That was the first time I had
         seen one. I had no idea. I had no idea that's what
         people did on their birthday. After that I never
         wanted one. I never felt that...

MARY: You should cut it. It's your cake, so go on and cut it,
         okay?

         GERRY picks up a knife.

         He looks to MARY. She motions for him to cut the cake.

         GERRY goes to cut in to the cake.

         Oh, hold on.

         She sings him a little bit of 'happy birthday', but peters out.

GERRY:

MARY: Go ahead.

         *He cuts the cake and then MARY takes over, putting a slice
         on a plate and passing it to him. She doesn't give herself a
         slice. GERRY eats.*

         MARY watches him eat.

         GERRY puts the cake down.

I have something else for you.

GERRY:

She places the small, blue Everton blanket on the table.

They both look at it. Neither says anything.

GERRY reaches out and touches it, but doesn't pick it up.

He looks at MARY.

MARY: Can you tell me... I'd like to know what it was like for you. What happened at the place they sent you to?

GERRY: The farm?

MARY: Was there anything good? Can you tell me something good?

GERRY: When I was... I don't know how old. On the farm. Years in to my time on the... And we... You know... We were meant to have school and stuff. A proper education, but it was never like that. It was just work. That's all I've ever known. Work. Kids as young as six or seven working the fields or with the cattle or whatever. Bare feet... bare hands... Burning hot days and freezing cold nights. Bad food... Bad clothes... Beatings. Beatings and... Hundreds of kilometres from any... Well, anything at all.

MARY: Beatings?

GERRY: There was a girl. Another... We didn't have much contact with the girls. They kept us all pretty separate. Different tables at mealtime. Different chores and jobs. Different sleeping quarters. It was really only now and then that we got to spend any time together. I don't know how this started. With me and her. But we would sneak out together. At night or... We'd each sneak out of our different sleeping quarters and we'd... We'd meet up and... Well, we'd hug each other. I don't mean... I mean there was nothing... I don't remember ever saying more than a word or two to her, and there wasn't anything... It was just like we wanted to hug each other. That was all. Just hugging. We'd meet. Hug for a while and then sneak back to our rooms. That was...

MARY:

GERRY: One of the adults found us this one time. All the kids were woken up and forced out of bed. All the adults were there. He had me. The head... Had hold of my arm as he told them all what I'd done. Pulled down my shorts. There were no underpants. We were never given underpants. And he caned me. In front of... Over and over. There in front of... Kicked me to the ground, too. Kicked me down and kept caning. Kept...

MARY:

GERRY: And her... She was gone by morning. I don't know where. She was just...

Silence.

MARY: And was there... Did anything else... Did anyone ever... Do anything to you, that...

GERRY:

GERRY reaches out for her hand, but again she doesn't take it.

What's going on?

MARY: I want to take you in my arms. I want to scoop you up and hold you here, next to my heart, as tightly as I can

They sit in silence.

Neither of them moves.

We see darkness.

END OF SCENE.

SCENE FOUR.

We see SALLY and MARK. They are in a hotel room, near Heathrow. They kiss, and then MARK breaks it.

MARK: How do you feel?

SALLY: A bit weird. Fine, thank you.

MARK: It's good to see you.

SALLY: I must look like a wreck.

MARK: Did you get my message?

SALLY: I haven't turned my phone on yet.

MARK: Of course.

SALLY: Is everything all right?

MARK: How's Gerry?

SALLY: He stormed up and down the isles the whole way.

MARK: Right.

SALLY: The attendants asked him to stop at one stage. He was keeping passengers awake. Then he just sat grumbling in the seat next to me.

MARK: Poor Gerry.

SALLY: But he'll be okay. You know how he is.

MARK: Shit.

SALLY: You seem… Are you sure everything's all right?

A toilet flushes.

MARK: Before he comes back, I should… Shit, I don't know how to do this.

SALLY: What is it?

MARK: Both of you… I just don't know how to

GERRY storms back in from the bathroom.

GERRY: Why are we in a hotel? Why aren't we going straight to Liverpool?

MARK: Gerry. Yes. How are you?

SALLY: Mark?

GERRY: What are we doing here?

MARK: You're probably feeling a bit weird. It will… It will take a day or two. To adjust. You're best to stay awake. I… Push through and try to go to bed at a normal… It'll be hard, but it'll save you days of trouble, when

GERRY: What are you talking about?

MARK: There's a park just near the hotel. A park and
          some cafes and things. I recommend getting some
          sunlight, if there is any today, and trying to stay
          awake as best you

SALLY: What's going on?

MARK: That goes for both of you.

GERRY: Why can't we just go straight up and see her?

MARK: You must both be exhausted. As I said, try to push
          through. Lots of... Lots of tea. Strong tea. Can I get
          you some? I should have done that already.

GERRY: I don't want any bloody tea. I'm sick of the stuff! I
          don't want to wait in this hotel room. I don't want
          to go to a bloody park. I want to go to Liverpool. I
          want to meet her and I want to do it now.

MARK: Sally filled you in, yeah?

GERRY: Or is she here? Have you brought her here? Is she
          in the hotel somewhere?

MARK: First... Thank you, Sal. I... That couldn't have been
          easy. Normally I would fly back and pass on the
          news myself, but because of time and things, I'd
          thought...

SALLY: What's wrong, Mark?

GERRY: Where is she? Another room? Is she here in another

MARK: I... I met her about a week ago. A little more. I met
          her up in Liverpool.

GERRY: And? Is she here?

MARK: Gerry…

GERRY: What?

MARK: Sal… Sally…

GERRY: What is it?

MARK: I didn't mean for it to go like this. I'm so…

GERRY: What's going on?

MARK: She's not here.

GERRY: Why not?

MARK:

GERRY: Mark?

SALLY: Oh no.

GERRY: What is going on?

MARK: We tried. We got you both here as quickly as we
         could.

SALLY: God.

GERRY: What do you mean?

MARK: We did everything we could.

GERRY: What's going on? Sally, what does he mean?

SALLY: Oh no.

GERRY: Stop that. Both of you. Stop saying… Someone tell
         me what's going on?!

MARK: Sally, I

GERRY: Can someone talk to me?!

MARK: Her name was Mary, Gerry. Mary Connor. I met her about a week ago and I could tell… It was obvious she still loved you. A lot.

GERRY: She what?

MARK: I'm sorry for how I've handled this.

GERRY: She died?

MARK: Yesterday.

GERRY:

MARK: She was determined to… She fought and fought, but

GERRY: No. You're saying… Don't… Sally, I don't get this. Help me, Sal? Why is he saying this? What is he saying? Jesus, someone tell me this isn't happening?!

Neither SALLY nor MARK can answer.

Mark, I'm begging you. I'm sorry. I know I've been a bastard. I know I've acted like a… But, please. Yeah?

SALLY: Dad…

GERRY: Please don't… Don't do this. Don't say this.

SALLY: Dad, stop.

GERRY: Please, God, don't say this?! Just let me… Just this once… I just need to be able to fucking

He picks up a lamp is about to throw it against the wall.

93

SALLY: Dad! No! Stop it! Don't do that!

          GERRY freezes. He looks at the object in his hands.

GERRY: I can't help... I can't hear... Look at me. Look at
          what's in me. This is who I am, right? This is what I
          deserve.

SALLY: Dad. Listen. This is the time to stop.

GERRY: But he's saying... But Sal, he's telling me that...

SALLY: And this is how you're going to react? Throwing
          something at the wall? Throwing it at one of us?!
          Taking it out on someone else?!

GERRY: I don't want to, but

SALLY: Then don't.

GERRY:

SALLY: You have a mother. I have a grandmother. She
          loved us. Think about that.

GERRY:

SALLY: Just put it down. That's all you have to do.

          GERRY puts the lamp down.

MARK: The funeral's in two days. Up in Liverpool. We'll...
          We'll arrange everything.

          To SALLY...

          She lay there and listened to me talk about you, Sal.
          She smiled. I held her hand and told her how...
          How beautiful you are... And kind... And... Well,
          anyway. She smiled this big, broad...

MARK pulls out a pile of letters and a CD, or memory stick.

To GERRY…

I have these, Gerry. She wrote to you. All the time. All those years. She wanted you to… She wrote these but never knew where to send them. Right up to the end she was writing them. We recorded her voice too. She wanted you to have them.

GERRY:

MARK: I'll leave you for a while. Leave you here to… Well, to look over things. Her things. Your things. I'll just put them here on the table. We'll take you up in the morning. Take the train up. It'll take a few hours. I'll take you to her home. Show you where

GERRY: No.

MARK: Sorry?

GERRY: Now. I want to go now. I don't want to wait. I'm sick of waiting.

MARK: Okay. Yes. Of course. You two have a shower… Do whatever you need to do, and I'll go and

GERRY: No. Let's go. Now.

SALLY: Dad, we should

GERRY: What? We should do what?

SALLY: All right. Let's go.

GERRY takes the letters and things in his arms, then he and SALLY pick their bags up. MARK steps in and picks SALLY's bag up for her. He reaches out to hold her hand, before…

Then we are nowhere. We just see GERRY and MARY.

MARY: I would get the bus to Aigburth. On my days off. I'd
         go over and sit in Sefton Park. We used to go there,
         you see. I used to take you over there to see what
         life should be like. We'd walk around and I'd make
         up stories for you about living in this house or that
         house. About the family we'd have. A father. Maybe
         a sister or brother for you. Silly stuff. It was really…

GERRY:

MARY: Well, once you were… After they'd taken you…
         I'd go and I'd watch these other families… These
         nice families. All in nice clothes and looking happy.
         Having little picnics, or playing, or… I used to look
         at the boys and try and find you. I thought I might
         be able to see him. You. I thought you might have
         just gone to a local family and that maybe I'd get to
         see you one day and I'd see how good things were
         for you and watch you play and that would be… If I
         got to do that, it would be

GERRY: Please, I

MARY: I thought I did one time. I thought I saw you.
         Just for a sec. Just as I got to the park a family
         was getting in to their car and this little boy was
         laughing and yelling as he got in the back seat. The
         laugh, it sounded just like… I ran over as they took
         off, hoping to get to see you, but… But the car… It
         drove off, and…

GERRY:

MARY: I went back whenever I could, hoping they'd come
         back. Hoping it was you. I've always hoped that boy
         was you, but…

GERRY: Stop, please.

MARY: When they built that cathedral. When it was being
built… At night… I used to go and throw rocks at it.
I'd throw rocks and scream at it and

GERRY: Stop.

Silence. MARY looks at the ground.

Why? Why did you go? I was on my way. I was
coming. I'm here. Look, I'm right here. Why didn't
you wait until I got here? You should have waited
until I…

MARY:

GERRY: Look at me. Please look at me.

She doesn't.

I thought you were dead. I spent my whole life
thinking you were dead, but that whole time… All
those years, you were here. You were here and…
And just…

MARY:

GERRY: I don't know who you are. I just want to know who
you are. I just need to get to see you, one time. If I
can do that, then…

MARY:

GERRY: Don't leave me. Please, don't

MARY disappears.

*GERRY is alone in the blackness. MARY's letters are in his
hands.*

We see GERRY and SALLY. They are in MARY's small flat. GERRY stands where MARY stood at the beginning of the play, and SALLY stands where GERRY stood.

There is silence.

GERRY: Can you… Can you come in?

SALLY: Are you sure?

GERRY:

SALLY: You don't want to be here alone?

GERRY: Please, can you come in?

SALLY moves closer to GERRY, in the middle of the room. They look over the small flat.

I don't… It means nothing to me. I don't recognise anything.

They look around the flat. Over a chair is the old, warn-out blue blanket. GERRY goes over and is going to pick it up, but stops himself.

I don't know. It doesn't feel right. Being here doesn't feel right.

SALLY looks at the pictures on the wall. She pulls one off and takes it back to GERRY.

SALLY: This must be you. You and her.

GERRY: What?

He takes the picture.

This is… You think this is me?

SALLY: You're so small.

GERRY: And this is her?

SALLY: I would get so angry with Mum every time she took you back. And then you'd do it all again. Over and over. 'Don't do it. Don't let him come back here' I'd want to scream it at her. I thought she was weak. I wanted to tell her. All the time. But I never… I didn't speak up. I didn't know how to…

GERRY:

SALLY: Why did you keep running off on us?

GERRY: I get low, Sal. Messed up. These things come back to me and… Your mother… I was like that when I… When I did it to her. So I started taking myself off. So I couldn't hurt you. Either of you. I do it so I can't…

SALLY: And you think that's going to solve anything?

GERRY: There are things, Sal. Things I don't know how to… Things that happened. Happened to me, and… I don't know how to tell you about them.

SALLY: Are you going to just keep running away and not dealing with them?

GERRY: I don't know what else to do.

SALLY:

GERRY: Why have you stuck with me?

SALLY: Mum was so alone. You were too. I don't want to live like that.

GERRY: She teased you about Mark, because the two of you are…

SALLY: But that doesn't mean that everything is…

GERRY:

SALLY: This is just the start. All this. You know that, don't you?

GERRY falls to his knees.

SALLY goes and holds him.

THE END

WWW.OBERONBOOKS.COM

Follow us on www.twitter.com/@oberonbooks
& www.facebook.com/OberonBooksLondon